TRANSIT

2015 - 2016
WITS ANTHOLOGY

Transit
2015-2016 WITS Anthology

©2016 Wordcrafters in Eugene

All Rights Reserved. This book may not be duplicated in any way—mechanical, photographic, electronic, or by means yet to be devised—without the written permission of the publisher, except in the case of brief excerpts or quotations for the purpose of review.

We are indebted to the program mentorship provided by Literary Arts in Portland, OR, especially to Mary Rechner, Mel Wells, and Andrew Proctor for their guidance and support.

Writers in the Schools is a program of Wordcrafters in Eugene, a non-profit literary arts organization whose mission is to provide writers and readers opportunities to strengthen their craft, deepen their connection with literature, and share their knowledge with each other and with future generations.

For more information please contact:
Wordcrafters in Eugene
438 Charnelton, Suite 102
Eugene, OR 97401
www.wordcraftersineugene.org

Sponsors

Business Sponsors

Meyer Memorial Trust
Eugene Metro Rotary
Luminare Press

Donors

Stacy Allen
Terry Brooks
Bill Cameron
Al and Liz Cratty
Vicki Elmer
Daryll Lynne Evans
George Filgate
Val Ford
Elizabeth George
Tracy Habecker
Elise Kimmons
Matt Lowes
Patricia Marshall
Juanita Metzler
Rex Moody
Kevin O'Brien
Susan Palmer
Susan Ploeger
Ellen Saunders
Janet Steward

Wordcrafters in Eugene

Staff

Daryll Lynne Evans, Executive Director
Sallie Vandagrift, WITS Coordinator

Board of Directors

Patricia Marshall, President
Elizabeth Engstrom Cratty
Christina Lay
Matt Lowes
Juanita Metzler
Wendy Morgan
Cheryl Owen Wilson

Anthology Staff

Editors: Daryll Lynne Evans and Sallie Vandagrift
Design: Luminare Press

Writers in the Schools

Writers-in-Residence

Jane Keyler, Rose Lambert-Sluder, Carter McKenzie,
Jake Powers, Charlie Schneider, Morgan Thomas,
Sallie Vandagrift, Leah Velez, and Cormac White

Visiting Authors

Myrlin Hepworth
Jacquelyn Mitchard

Participating Teachers

Caroline Comerford, Thurston High School
Trish Robison, Phoenix Program at
John Serbu Youth Campus

Introduction

Dear Readers,

In just three short years, Wordcrafters in Eugene has built a strong foundation for our Writers in the Schools (WITS) program. Since its launch, the WITS program has served nearly 2000 students in six school districts, including schools in rural and under-served areas. The focus has been to provide opportunities and quality programming for young writers to learn and practice their craft.

Each spring, WITS brings national best-selling authors, such as Gail Tsukiyama and Jacquelyn Mitchard, to speak to high school students in Springfield and Eugene about their books and what it is like to be a professional writer. In the fall we bring nationally recognized spoken word artist Myrlin Hepworth to rural schools for spoken word poetry performances and writing workshops.

WITS also offers a Young Writers Fiction Contest, open to all students in Lane County. Winners are presented at the Wordcrafters annual Writing Festival, Be Writing.

Because learning and creating don't stop when school's out, WITS also holds No-School Creative Camps, where young writers get to explore the intersection of art and creative writing, as well as Summer Creative Writing Camps, where young writers get to explore different modes and genres of writing with a different professional writer each day.

Most notably for the 2015-2016 school year, we were able to launch our WITS Writers Residency Series, which places professional writers in Lane County classrooms. These residencies give students the opportunity to work alongside a professional writer over the course of five to eight-weeks as part of their school day. Students get to explore creative writing with a focus on the whole writing process, from composition through drafting, revising, polishing, and finally public performance and publication; creating a bridge to stronger writing and stronger academic performance across the curriculum. Studying alongside a professional writer gives students the opportunity to see what professional writing looks like up close. It also helps students to find their voice and empowers them to tell their stories.

Our Writers-in-Residence for 2015-2016 were poet Carter McKenzie and WITS Coordinator and writer Sallie Vandagrift. Carter visited two classrooms at Thurston High School for an intensive study of poetry and poetic forms. Sallie led three residencies at the Phoenix Program at the the John Serbu Youth Campus. She was assisted by graduate students in the Master of Fine Arts program for creative writing at University of Oregon.

We hope you enjoy this collection of writing from the many participants of this year's WITS programs. This anthology illustrates that no matter where you have been or where you are going, the power of your voice is valuable tool for inspiration and vision. The participants of WITS reveal in their writing a capacity for imagination, vulnerability, and possibility that deserves to be heard. Read on!

Sincerely,

Daryll Lynne Evans, Executive Director
Sallie Vandagrift, WITS Coordinator

Contents

Sponsors	iii
Wordcrafters in Eugene Staff	iv
Writers in the Schools	v
Introduction	vi

Kristin Conrad
    Memories … 1

Anice Teel
    The Night … 2

Amina Z. Donahoe
    Listening to the Growth … 3

Kalvin Freese
    Heartbroken … 4

Trish Robison
    Blue Song … 5

Celia Sherman
    Abigail … 6

Abrial Vinson
    Famous Things … 8

Ryan Corgain
    Strawberries … 9

Melissa Rendsland
    The Old … 10

Kaylin Salladay
    Paths to my House or Home … 11

Ella Schmeling
    When a Meerkat Moves to the City … 12

Morgan Thomas
> SISTER — 20

Katie F.
> PERHAPS — 21

Iris Bartholomew
> EXCERPT FROM "OFFICE HOURS" — 23

Ashleigh Ward
> RED DEER — 25

Anika Foy
> LETTERS AND CORN CHIPS — 26

Kendall Minium
> THE FAMOUS GAME — 31

Grace Foltz
> GOVERNMENT AFFAIRS — 32

Angelique Hoffman
> I WANT — 38

Trish Robison
> GERALD — 39

Anice Teel
> EARLY MORNING — 40

Madison Smith
> PIECE NAME — 41

Paige Davis
> ALIVE — 42

Rylan Larsen
> A DREAM AT DEATH'S DOOR: THE LONG FLIGHT — 43

Melissa Rendsland
> I BELIEVE — 51

Dan Renteria
 BORING   52

Matthew Johnson
 CONCENTRATION   53

Blake McKay
 BE   54

Angelique Hoffman
 BLIND DIRECTIONS   55

Alex Johnson
 RESTLESSNESS   56

Charlie Schneider
 EXCERPT FROM "HEYDAY"   57

Matthew Johnson
 DEER OF STONE   61

Parker B. Rook
 DREAD   62

Paige Davis
 MY LIFE TO BE   63

Doran Simpson
 CONFUSION   64

Abrial Vinson
 FIVE DIRECTIONS TO MY HOUSE   65

Sander Moffitt
 SEEKING THE HIDDEN   66

Carter McKenzie
 WHAT MUST BE TRUE   76

Kristin Conrad
Thurston High School, 12th Grade

Memories

The snow has a certain sense of purity.
The hills white and storm-hit,
Animals trying to remember how to walk through it.

Times with my family going up to stay in our storm-hit cabin.
Back in a time of purity and light

Where my laughter, heart, and world were pure.
Realizing not only were the mountains storm-hit, but so was my life.
Every time I see the snow I remember that time.

Anice Teel
Thurston High School, 12th Grade

The Night

Under all the
Netting of the stars
In warm embraces
Vibrations of croaking frogs
Evergreens swaying in the breeze
Roaming minds
Soft caresses
Everything at peace

Inspired by "Universe" by Steven Schnur

Amina Z. Donahoe
Thurston High School, 12th Grade

Listening to the Growth

The grass grows slow
unclear to the naked eye.
How long has the green grass grown,
In the quiet yard
the ants below
form marching bands
made of trumpets and trombones
Above the birds scream
of yet another wakening
of the sun
The smell of the orange
from the light of day
Tells the infinite story
Of green grass growing

Kalvin Freese
Thurston High School, 12th Grade

Heartbroken

A cloudy overcast sky spanning far and wide
A glimmering ray of hope at the end of a tunnel
The world keeps spinning as ours starts to slow
To nothing but a crawl
We still exist but our lives portray nothing at all

Trish Robison

Classroom Teacher, Phoenix Program
John Serbu Youth Campus

Blue Song

She went to the biggest store
On one of the biggest blocks
And opened up the heavy purple door
Thinking of brand new purple socks
The thing that happened next
Was surprising and wonderful and true
Her body became covered in text
Every song she ever loved, it was blue
Why was this the moment for this thing
Why was this the place
Turns out it was time for her heart to sing
Turns out she had lost the race

Celia Sherman
Edison Elementary, 4th Grade

Abigail

Abigail is a 9-year-old girl. She goes to Edison Elementary School. Abigail was sitting at her desk at school. She was so bored. She hated writing. Reluctantly, she headed her paper, May 6, 1936. She started to write. "I love sugar. My life is boring. All I really want is for something to happen in my life and I also want to *buy* my dresses. My mother is a seamstress so I get all my dresses from her."

One day Abigail saw someone go into a place. It was dark and there were lots of things lining the walls. It was very dusty. After the person left she ran in before the door closed. She caught the door and went in. There were loads of awesome stuff in there, even a baby pool. She kept walking. Then she saw a bag with some cookies in it. At first she was cautious about eating them, but then she saw what was written on the bag: May 2, 1936. "Oh," she said, "they are only four days old." She picked up the bag and started eating.

Just as she finished the last cookie a weird feeling came to her stomach. Suddenly her legs became weak. She closed her eyes and fell asleep for the last time. Abigail had been poisoned. But, like all people after death, she could make a choice! She made the decision to stay as close as possible to living. She became a ghost. She did everything like the life had never left her body. She did all the homework that was due, she played in the little space she had in the catacombs.

She even caught, killed, and tried to eat food, but of course she couldn't to eat food.

Eighty years, longer than her living years, went by. She didn't have many visitors. It was February 2, 2016 and Abigail realized that it was almost her death day when PEOPLE came in. Yes, people, not a person but People! There were seven of them. Five were kids her age and two were adults. That surprised Abigail. She had never seen five kids in there at once. She hid and she watched them. She followed them out. She watched them write about her home. She watched them write about what they thought she was like. She watched them write letters to her and stories about her. She liked the attention even if it wasn't direct. She decided she would watch them and maybe let them see her face.

Abrial Vinson
Thurston High School, 12th Grade

Famous Things

Peonies
Lilies
Daisies
Sunflowers
Hydrangeas
Tulips
Orchids
Violets
Lavender
Azaleas
Camellias
Poppies
Witch Hazel
Irises
Jade
Jasmine
Pansies
All flowers are famous for being beautiful by nature
And not by man

Inspired by "Famous" by Naomi Shihab Nye

Ryan Corgain

Thurston High School, 12th Grade

STRAWBERRIES

S mooth in a shake
T asty in a salad
R ight for every occasion
A rranged with any fruit
W ell that's why they're so great
B ut never eat bananas, that is forever bad luck
E very time you eat one your happiness will grow
R emembering the last time you ate one
R ight now you want one
I think you need one
E ven its greatness is measured like Jordan's
S o be like Nike and just do it

Melissa Rendsland
Thurston High School, 12th Grade

The Old

The old have lived through.
Their souls are ragged and old,
They have taken their time to live,
Have picked their mountains and gone through.
Slowly their tiredness seeps through.
Young acting as old,
Frightened to live,
Pushed to the edge to live,
Finally they come through
Sleepy and cold and old.

Kaylin Salladay
Thurston High School, 12th Grade

Paths to my House or Home

1. Follow the path ahead for it will bring you here.
2. Pass the houses with the greenest of grass and freshest of paints for you are far from the place labeled home.
3. Continue on, steady with each step, until your feet leave the fresh gray pavement and enter the rough uneven cracks of my streets.
4. Stay opposite of the yellow dead field for no one knows what lies there.
5. When you reach the brown strong walls of my house, stand silently and question: Is this my house or my home?

Ella Schmeling
Holt Elementary, 4th grade

When a Meerkat Moves to the City

Oscar is a fancy Meerkat who is yearning for a home. He was always a little different from his family. Each day he wears a black shimmering top hat with a red bow tie on his neck that shows the true charm of Oscar. Oscar used to live in Africa but he thought it was too wild for him. He always wonders why it is so wild? Oscar once tried to ask someone why it's so crazy around here and he almost got eaten alive. That was when he knew not to talk to strangers. A while after Oscar realized he could not stay there. He wandered off to the city to find the perfect home. He hoped the new strangers he met wouldn't be as mean. Luckily there shouldn't be lions in the city.

While he was traveling on his journey he found a sign that said Barn House. Oscar jumped with excitement and said, "This sounds like a great home. I shall go check it out." Oscar straightened his bow tie and headed towards the barn. He tried really hard to dodge the soggy brown mud that was everywhere on the ground. He did not want his silky fur to get muddy. Oscar saw a big fence with some sort of creature on the other side. He climbed up to the top and saw, well he had no clue what he saw. Oscar politely said, "Good day sir. What a lovely morning," while he tipped his hat and smiled.

The creature's response was "MOO!!!"

He said, "Excuse me I think you misunderstood what I said."

"MOO!!!!!!" it said again.

Oscar shouted, "No we are not on the MOON!" Frustrated, Oscar hopped onto the creature's back to get his attention but it moo'ed so loudly that Oscar shouted even louder this time, "Listen to me, you Moo-mammal!" Oscar thought it was beginning to become pointless to talk to this creature.

Oscar began to wonder if the city was really the best place for him to seek a new home. Africa was too far away for him to journey back so his only choice was to keep going. While lonely searching for a place to call home, Oscar smelled a horrid stench. "Pee-yew, I should not be around such a smell." He quickly scampered on his way, as far away from that odor as possible, trying to imagine what his new home would be like. It surely would have gold and priceless possessions with the fanciest food anyone could imagine.

As he was walking away he heard an old rattily scratchy voice calling, "Hey, you! I'm walking here, watch your step buddy!" Oscar did not appreciate this attitude but part of his charm was not just being the best dressed Meerkat in town, he was also raised to be the most polite Meerkat. He answered nicely, "Excuse me, what is your name?"

"I'm Ratty."

Oscar couldn't help but notice that Ratty was a rat. "What an interesting name for a rat," Oscar thought. He realized that everybody around here should have a home so he asked, "Where do you live, Mr. Ratty?"

Ratty pointed at the garbage can that Oscar was purposely trying to avoid because of the horrible odor. Oscar laughed, "What a great sense of humor you have! Can you imagine a silver tinted smelly garbage can could be someone's home?"

The rat responded in a grouchy voice, "You think this is a joke? I live here! These garbage cans have been in my family for generations! Kids!!! Come out here and meet our guest, Oscar the Meerkat." The three little rats hopped out of the garbage can and said, with no manner at all, "Hi I am Suzie," the oldest of the rat children said while licking her fingers, having just eaten lunch. "And these are my little brothers, Joseph and Tom." Joseph and Tom waved at Oscar.

Ratty invited Oscar over for dinner. Being so polite, Oscar would never turn down an invitation for a meal. Besides, he was hungry. After all, it had been a long time since he'd eaten. Joseph brought him in and sat him down at his chair. Ratty was in the kitchen preparing the food while Oscar sat nicely and tucked his napkin into his bow tie. Finally, Ratty was done and handed what looked like fish carcass over to Oscar. He could not help but to almost yack in his mouth, but being so well mannered he ate the food while holding his breath, hoping no one would notice. After he was done with his meal he said his goodbyes and went on his way. He didn't want to stick around for dessert, who knows what that could be!

"This seems hopeless," Oscar groaned while walking and looking at the rugged ground. Oscar ran into a building. He looked up and saw a sign that said Home Depot. "Maybe this is where I can find my forever home!"

He walked proudly into the building while smiling at every person he saw. The people smiled at him too, it was an odd smile though. Oscar did not find very many homes there but still continued searching. In one of the isles he saw a gray metal tube he could fit right into. Oscar hopped into the tube and didn't think it was that comfortable. "Well, maybe it needs some getting used to," Oscar said with a sigh.

He went off looking for supplies for his new home. He noticed the garden section and saw a beautiful flower that would make the tube smell very fragrant, it was colorful too. Just the thing to brighten up his tube. Oscar definitely needed to find furniture to match this flower. While looking for a comfortable seat, Oscar saw purple duct tape that would complement the yellow petunia in the tube. Next to the duct tape were short sticks that he could make into a chair with the use of the duct tape. He went back to his home only to find that it was missing and the flower was left on the ground all crumpled. Oscar looked towards the place where his tube was with worry, "Ugh, I shall make another one." Oscar saw another tube that looked exactly the same on the shelf right behind where the first one was. He gathered the supplies and started to get to work on his new home. When his new home was finally finished he laid down for an evening rest.

By being startled awake, Oscar realized he was being carried away. He shrieked, "Ahhhhhhh!" No one heard a thing because he was so small and the fact that the tube was sound proof did not help. Oscar leaped to the ground with his top hat perfectly landing on his head. Although discouraged, he straightened his bow tie and walked away. "Am I ever going to find a place of my own?" He said with a slight tear.

It was growing dark and Oscar knew he had to go to bed, but it was awful hard to get to sleep without a bedtime story and a nice cozy blanket to cuddle with. He decided to tell himself a tall tale and used a leaf that had fallen on to the ground from the tree above him as blanket. Even though the leaf was soggy and wet and the bed time story was one he'd heard time and time again he finally drifted off to sleep.

Oscar woke up at the crack of dawn and feared he was never going to find a home, but he had no idea what was coming up ahead. Frustration and anger got the best of him and he threw his hat as far as he could. "I WILL NEVER FIND THE PERFECT HOME!!!" he shouted as he stomped his feet up and down. All of a sudden his hat appeared like a boomerang and landed perfectly back on his head. Surprised, Oscar threw the hat again with all of his might. It just so happened that this time the hat hit the edge of the tree. Oscar saw something fall from the tree and into his hat. He ran over and saw what was in it.

A tiny voice called, "Please don't hurt me Mister Meerkat, I am only a little field mouse."

Oscar looked at the mouse with suspicion, "Hurt you? I'd never do such a thing."

The field mouse called out again, "You wouldn't? Are you sure? You seem to have quite the temper."

"No, I'm just feeling a bit frustrated because I cannot find a home."

"Me too!" cried the mouse. "Do you want to work together to find a perfect home?"

Oscar nodded with pleasure, feeling slightly embarrassed that someone saw him lose his composure, the cheeks on his face turned red. The two ventured off, seeking a home.

Oscar and Sheila, the field mouse, enjoyed having each other as company. It was nice to have someone else that understood exactly what the other was thinking and feeling. As they began their search together they heard a very loud noise, so loud it made the ground tremble. They looked up to find a ginormous metal bird flying in the sky. Now who has heard of a metal bird?

"What was that?" Sheila asked. Oscar shrugged his shoulders, "I don't know, do you want to go check it out?" Of course Sheila said yes.

They walked onto a runway where they saw many of the other large birds. Sheila also spotted someone that looked an awful lot like Oscar. They walked towards this man who had a black top hat that matched his suit with a gleaming red bow tie. He was carrying a suitcase. Oscar and Sheila were very curious what was in this strangely large suitcase. Without being noticed, Oscar unzipped the zipper of the bag and they peered in. The man just so happened to zip it back up with Sheila and Oscar inside.

Sheila had a big fear of tight spaces and began to panic. "Oh no, I'm so scared!"

Oscar held Sheila's hand and smiled trying to comfort her, but that was the least of their troubles. They suddenly began to feel that they were moving at a great speed. They instantly became dizzy and dozed off to sleep.

When they woke up they unzipped the bag hoping to escape and saw a giant load of boxes with bags of peanuts and pretzels that were full of wonder!!!! They were awfully hungry after their unexpected flight so they slipped into a couple of bags, well, maybe more than a couple. Oscar found a bottle of soda that looked delightful and took a chug. He had a big burp and gasped, "My heavens, what is this?" Sheila giggled.

Finally, they were able to get off the plane. Their eyes hurt when walking outside to the bright light of the summer sky. As their eyes adjusted Sheila and Oscar saw something unimaginable to see!!!! Oscar and Sheila saw a castle made of gold and shiny bronze with many guards standing around it. Oscar barely could believe himself. "Are you seeing this too!!!???"

Sheila couldn't answer, her mouth was stuck wide open with surprise. Oscar knew exactly what she was thinking. They knew they would have to be very clever to find a way past the guards and into the castle so they tip toed in that direction. Tip toe, tip toe, tip toe.

They made their way to the castle and realized there was no way for them to sneak in without the guards noticing. Their best idea was to go to the front entrance and introduce themselves to the guards. After all, Oscar had a way with manners. They each put on their best smile, stood up straight just like the guards were doing and greeted them.

"Good day sir," Oscar said with a tip of his top hat and a straightening of his bow tie. The guard just stood still and didn't seem to notice.

"Are all these city folks going to ignore me all the time?" He remembered the first time he greeted someone in the city and it didn't go so well. Maybe "moo" is the only word these people like to use. Oscar smiled and said, "Mooooooooo."

He finally got a look from one of the guards, a strange look which turned into a laugh. Apparently a guard had never seen a sophisticated Meerkat that says moo. Soon after the guard's little giggle, he stood straight back up while getting back to work.

The guards didn't seem to care so much about a Meerkat and a Mouse walking into the castle so they went on their way right past them. They walked into a big castle with beautiful possessions and fancy people of all sorts. Sheila's feet were getting awfully tired from all of their walking so Oscar let her take a ride on top of his hat, which was shimmering from the lights in the castle.

Oscar felt a grip like he was being carried away. In fact, that was exactly what was happening. Oscar looked up and saw a little girl with curly blonde hair and big blue eyes. Her smile was brighter than any sunshine. Sheila waved at this little girl. The girl waved back and called, "Mommy, Daddy!

I found two new pets!" Oscar and Sheila's faces blew up with excitement. They didn't know what to say so they just smiled at each other.

The parents were a little confused with the arrival of their daughter's new pets but nodded as a way of saying she could keep them. The little girl screamed and twirled her pink sparkly dress.

"Fiona, you know what we talked about, no screaming in the castle!" Her dad reminded her. She knew better but was so happy she couldn't contain herself.

Fiona had the best Barbie houses and clothes that she knew would fit Oscar and Sheila perfectly. She brought them to her room and dressed Oscar in a black tuxedo with the top hat and bow tie that he was already wearing. Sheila got to wear a beautiful dress with a lovely pearl necklace. They shortly figured out that Fiona was throwing them a fancy ball to celebrate them joining their family. Although this was their first ball, Oscar and Sheila knew they'd have many more enjoyable celebrations like this such as birthday parties, weddings, and tea parties with fancy dinners.

The very next morning, Fiona sat them down at the dinner table and Queen Bellafina and King Clarion gave them a delicious pancake breakfast. This was just the life Oscar was dreaming of. Oscar learned something on this very special journey of trying to find his perfect home. It's not just about the fancy house you get, it's the people you share it with.

Morgan Thomas

Writer in Residence
Phoenix Program at John Serbu Youth Campus

Sister

My sister is sausage gumbo
she won't eat—
white rice curdled with roux
we whisked in a Caphalon pot,
and she is the pot itself
with scores in the base
where food sticks,
those scratches
from our flat whisk always
scraping against bone.

Katie F.
Thurston High School, 12th Grade

Perhaps

Perhaps I should return those
Remaining sands
Back to cool beaches, and let them return
There, to the winds.
Instead, let's keep them close at hand,
    my secret collection of
Seashells.

Perhaps I am the waves, returning to the same place
Again and again
Repeating the scenes, lest I forget,

Perhaps I am a bird, following the winds wherever
    they may lead me

We may come from different elements.
The sands of time may change us
Further on,
But we are still of the land
I would rather be here, in these moments by the
    shores, until
I must go

Onward, to be a seed in the wind once again.

In this way, we relate
In this way I can speak with little revealed
Or perhaps, already, it pours of the pages like rain.
Please, come, oh wind, lest I fade uncertain.
May I know that these mere
Sandstorms only bring us closer
So I can return, toward that long,
    vast place once again.

Iris Bartholomew
North Eugene High School, 9th Grade

Excerpt from "Office Hours"

His boots scuffed the floors of the office building, leaving behind dark marks wherever his shoes had been. He walked along, passing officials and service reps, all insidious workers with dapper suits and ties. He was dapper in his own way; not in his looks, (broad shoulders, shifty eyes,) but in his charm. Such charm got him into concerts, out of jail, and off the map. Now, this man's charm was getting him to the fifteenth floor of Chapman and Buckle Industries. His lungs were not as they used to be, however, so midway down the hall corridor of the third floor, his breathing began to diminish. His eyes wandered, mouth agape, locking on the elevator. He started towards his destination, charm in hand.

Ten steps later, he was at the elevator, just as the doors began to creak shut. He sped up his loose footsteps, and reached the doors just in time for a man in a black suit to grasp the door, and pull it open.

"Thank you, sir," the man stuttered blankly, leaning his body against the railing of the patchy elevator.

The man in the suit shrugged, and moved to the back of the elevator. After he caught his breath, the man decided to survey his surroundings: a ragged girl in a coffee-stained black ensemble, frowning into her phone, a man, his mind as fragile as glass slippers, the man that opened the door, and a woman with fiery hair and a lopsided smile.

    The elevator was close to the top floor not much later, causing the man to smile. His hand reached for the emergency button, yellow as a lemon under his fingertips. Without hesitation, he pushed it. The elevator lurched to a stop, and everyone froze.

    Screams of confusion, gasps of unclear realizations, and a smiling man near the front. This time, his wits had lead him right where he wanted to be. He had rehearsed the moment many times, but it felt better to live it.

    "It's all right," he whispered, providing an empty comfort to the aura of the room. The comfort ceased soon, however.

    That was when he reached into the bellows of his pocket, and pulled out the gun.

Ashleigh Ward
Thurston High School, 12th Grade

Red Deer

The red deer is covered in blood.
He has lived long
and is very strong.
Through my scope I see
he is beautiful
but we're here to hunt.
My tag has not been filled
and he is a wide target.
The gunfire stings my ears,
while I lay
watching him.
He falls and my heart breaks.
I hear my father and brother cheering
although I feel guilty
I am also proud
Sorry for the life I have just taken
but glad I can pursue mine.

Anika Foy
Roosevelt Middle School, 7th Grade

Letters and Corn Chips

I stare at the thin white paper in my hand. My fist closes around it, crinkling the once pristine, perfect fluorescent white sheet. I notice with satisfaction the tearing sound that it makes as the torque on some small bits and pieces becomes too much for the frail sheet to bear. This definitely helps, but only a little bit. Not enough for me to truly feel okay, to be fine with this. I hear the swish of fabric behind me, feel my mother's gentle hand settle onto my trembling shoulder. She starts to massage my shoulder, and then makes as if to hug me. I suddenly despise her, her decision, her *grit* to make that movement. I don't need her pity. She doesn't get to see me like this, a small, weak little child. This doesn't involve her in the slightest. Every muscle in my body tenses, trying to keep the wave of angry-sad tears in -to no avail. My eyes burning, the first drop already making its way down my clammy cheek, I jerk away and sprint for the stairs, my long brown hair whipping around and trailing behind me, taking the steps two at a time and then slamming the door to my room. I flop down onto the plush comfort of my bed. It feels as if there's a boulder in my throat. No, scratch that. It feels as if there's an entire *planet* in my throat. I stare at my ceiling. The neon pink poster duct taped there, a smiling gray striped kitten sporting a pink sweater and hipster glasses, mocks me: "Chin up!"

Chin up, my ass. Everyone always says, "Oh, it'll get better," until *they're* in a bad situation. I press my arms to my sides and squeeze, anything to stop these waterworks. I hear a soft crinkle. Salty tears still streaming down my face, I realize that I'm clenching the letter. My letter. Suddenly, I can't fathom why I crumpled it. It's not my dad's fault. He's just busy at work in his new, grand home that he tells me about. Heck, in the few letters he sends, he says that he sees movie stars there daily, even stays in beautiful hotel rooms just for the fun of it! I should be happy for him, not all selfish and hurt that he can't make it to my silly little half-birthday party. Stupid rollercoaster of emotions. I gently unfold the letter, read the words scrawled in his practically illegible inky handwriting that marches across the page like little black spiders. Again… And again… And again. And oh, did I mention that I read it another time after that?

"Sorry, champ. Can't come visit this year. Maybe next? Love, Dad." This letter gets tucked where all the rest do, in the shoebox under my bed. It's kinda like a graveyard for dead wishes, when you think about it. Woah, morbid. Just what you'd expect from my messed up, self-centered mind that blames people for being happy and busy. Again, not my dad's fault. He's a busy man, with his new job and all. As I stand from my kneeling position on the floor, pushing the box of letters back under my bed with a stockinged foot, I hear the soft rat-a-tat-tat- of knocking at my door. I wipe my face, though that act is fruitless. The tears have dried there already anyways, a shiny, crusty shell over my reddened cheeks.

"What?" I call, trying to keep my voice level, passive, and even. I fail. It's all cracky and dry, like an old woman's. It's aggressive as well, like I'd like nothing more in the world than for her to go away. Damn it. So much for pretending

I'm fine. I curse under my breath, and my mother peeks in. "Hmm?" She asks.

"Nothing," I mumble, looking down at the plush carpeted floor of my bedroom. She makes as if to speak again, like she wants to say more, but just ends up closing her mouth, letting the words die on her lips. She turns away and walks downstairs, leaving me wondering whether or not I should run to catch her or not. I don't.

BEEP. BEEP. BEEP. The sound of my blaring alarm is like a sledgehammer smashing into my skull every time it rings. I moan and roll over, wiping crusty bits of drool off of the corner of my mouth as I push up off of the bed with a grunt. Yeah, I'm basically a savage in the morning. (Cue that Pocahontas song about savages).

I look through my closet in disgust. What grade am I in, second? I make a mental note to go shopping with Kirstie sometime soon, maybe go to Forever 21 or H&M. Kirstie is my best friend, a.k.a. most awesome person ever. We do everything together, whether it's going out to eat, watching a movie, or even just lazing about. When I broke my ankle on my eigth birthday at SkatePlanet, she was there for me. Drama, she's on it. Relationship troubles? She's there for me to lean on. She's the best.

Anyways, I eat breakfast, get to school, all that jazz. It's all boring stuff (who even needs algebra?) until right after the last bell rings. Kirstie catches up to me on my way out of the scratched up forest green doors whose rusty hinges creak each time a child pushes out of them, pushed and pulled in the current of rushing, B.O. smelling adolescents. Yeah, high school's great.

"Macy! You sooo need to come to the party at my place

this weekend! It's gonna be off the hoooook!" She lets out a loud whoop and starts bouncing on the balls of her feet, staring eagerly at me, waiting for a response.

"Uh, sure! Anyone interesting gonna be there?" I ask. By that, of course, I mean, "Will Thomas be there?" She knows that, I'm sure, judging by the devilish look spreading over her face.

"Ah, yes, I invited him *especially* for you." She giggles with an impish grin.

"Count me in, then," I chuckle, my expression matching hers. Why not? Thomas is cute, and I think he likes me. We walk hand in hand towards my house for a while until her mother pulls up to the curb next to us, and she departs with a cheery wave my way.

Party. Dad. Party. Dad. Party. This is what runs through my mind as I stare, once again, at that stupid cat poster above my bed. I've begun to hate that smiling, optimistic cat. I don't care to go into detail, so I'll just say this: he's in prison. My dad, that is, not the cat. I don't even know that cat's gender. Anyway, soon after mom and he got divorced, he got into gambling, got into a lot of trouble. This was all explained to me in a letter. He sent me a freaking *letter* to tell me that everything he's been telling me about, how the movie stars and the mansions, the palm trees and cozy hotel rooms, are lies. All of them. And now he wants me to visit him in prison this weekend. He wants me to visit him? In prison? What the hell went through his mind when he was writing this? Fathers can't just tear down their daughters' worlds like this. It's horrible, disgusting, really. I can't believe this. I don't want to believe this.

And yet…I want to see him. I don't even remember what he looks like, what he sounds like, what his hugs feel like.

Mom got rid of all of our pictures of him after their big fight. Nothing related to him is in our house anymore, having been all thrown out in a tearful, though reasonable, fit or rage on my mother's part. All I can remember of him is the smell of stale corn chips. The ones that people forget about until they clean out their old, dusty cupboards. These people taste one bit of a chip from the spoiled bag and throw them away in disgust. Then I realize two vital things: He threw me away, and he threw my mom away. My brave, proud mother who'd risk everything for me, I'm sure. He threw everything away. He threw his whole damn *life* away. So now I'll throw him away, throw him out of my life. I'm going to go to that party of Kirstie's and I'm going to *love* it. And I will never, *ever* respond to that letter.

    He never writes me again.

Kendall Minium
Thurston High School, 12th Grade

The Famous Game

Cristiano Ronaldo is famous to the game of soccer,
just like Mia Hamm is famous everywhere.
I want to be famous like them,
a good role model to others.
I praise the cleats I get and the time on the field.
Each day I wake up wanting to feel the burn
of the hot turf coming through my cleats,
the sweat dripping from my face,
and the sight of the terrible soccer tan lines
on a scorching summer day.
You never know, but there are many
athletes younger than you wanting
to be like you, training hard every day.
I want to be famous to those who
can't do what I'm able to do.
I want to make them proud like my family,
who know that I am not just going through
the motions because I can, but
taking advantage of every moment
knowing each day could be the last.
It is a BLESSING.

Inspired by "Famous" by Naomi Shihab Nye

Grace Foltz
Ridgeline Montessori School, 8th grade

Government Affairs

The other kids were eating my dust, well...air. Sure, the beginning boards they had put us on didn't go higher than one foot off the ground. That didn't mean I couldn't cruise as fast as I wanted on them. Although my speed may have had something to do with the tampering I had done with the safety controls. I wasn't technically supposed to be going this fast, it being my first year at the academy and all. But who was it hurting? Surely not myself. My titanium frame would keep me safe from all but a few cracked solar panels on my "skin," and, as long as they didn't break off, that was nothing I couldn't fix.

The instructor's "Slow down!" was muffled by the wind rushing by my sound intakes. I could hear her next shout more clearly: "The strip ends soon!"

She was referring to the strip of magnets that ran underneath the ground. Without them, the magnets in the hoverboards would have nothing to repel against.

I did some quick calculations in my head. After figuring out that the strip should go on for a few more miles, I surged ahead.

It's true that insubordination wasn't usually my M.O. Josie and Viv had programmed me better than that. But there was just something about hoverboarding that made my wires go a little haywire. Call it a glitch. Of course, it could also just be a reaction to my close proximity with the magnets beneath me.

I had left behind the frozen plains of the Academy grounds a while ago. Great mountains of glittering ice replaced them as I neared the Pacific shore.

I closed my eyes. That was, after all, what most humans seemed to do when they were surrounded with beautiful things. Why, I'm not sure. How do you experience the view if you can't even see it? My logical thinking didn't understand. My Human Interactions and Emotions program did...kind of.

The board jerked and shuddered beneath me before it promptly threw me off. I had ran out of strip.

I landed hard on the ice, but, as I expected, it was nothing my titanium frame couldn't handle. By the time I had gotten to my feet, the slick ice had lured me down again. Before I knew it, I was rolling down an incline, rolling until I landed in a small gorge with a thunk.

The sound surprised me. I had expected the noise to be classified as ice, but my sound recognition software identified it as a thick slab of iron. Everything looked like ice. My sound recognition software, though, was one of the few programs that rarely malfunctioned. Testing out the surface was probably worthwhile.

I tapped my knuckles on the wall of the gorge. The sound that followed was definitely not one of ice.

I pushed against the wall but nothing happened. Luckily, my left index finger was equipped with a lasercutter. I only needed to wait for the synthetic nail bed to slide back before carving a jagged hole in the wall.

The darkness that greeted me once the slab fell through wasn't completely unexpected.

Fortunately my night vision was designed for situations like this.

Hundreds of black-screened monitors lined the walls of a room. The space was void of people. I cautiously stepped inside. Instantly overhead lights blinked on, as if being awakened after a long night's sleep, and I got a better view of the room.

It was maybe the size of a classroom at the Academy. An abundance of desks, machinery, and papers were strewn throughout the room, leaving only a few small paths.

I followed a path that lead to one of the bigger monitors. Hesitantly, I pressed the tips of my fingers against it. With a flash, the monitor sprang to life. A green light swept across it, most likely activated by a pressure sensor. Finding no fingerprints, the entire screen turned red:

INTRUDER ALERT! INTRUDER ALERT! INTRUDER ALERT!

Oops.

I tapped frantically against the screen trying to stop the alarm. Nothing worked. Years of advanced code and computer science training and I couldn't stop a stupid alarm.

I knew my Human Interactions and Emotions program was overriding when my fist slammed against the screen. That's what snapped me back to my senses. If I calmed down enough to let my logical thinking take charge—got it.

I reached back and dug a fingernail into the nape of my neck. The panels there slid away to reveal a coiled USB cord. The nearest port I could find was on the side of a monitor to my left.

I tugged the cord to meet it. Then, I set to work.

I logically assumed that I was not welcome here and could be in big trouble. The least I could do was find out for what.

While, try as I might, I hadn't been able to shut off the alarm, I hacked into their data files with ease. It didn't take me long to figure out the name of the project: C.H.I.L.L. That didn't tell me much. I dug deeper.

Large sums of money from various government departments, signed contracts, treaties, and, finally, a mission statement dating back to when the Academy was founded nearly twenty years ago. Photos of cities with thick smog, rivers flooding, dried up lakes, and melting ice caps blazed across the screen. A picture of the Academy's wind turbines was last. Puzzled, I clicked on it.

Blueprints of the turbines popped up. But, the designs didn't match up. According to the blueprints, the turbines were actually pumping out $Co2$, instead of converting wind into electrical energy. By now, I was quite sure I had finally figured out what a "bad feeling" was. I kept searching the database. My attention was drawn to a secure email from an Army general named James Tolen. It was encrypted, but so were my memory files. I knew what to do.

In minutes I was reading Tolen's letter. It referred to the successful establishment of C.H.I.L.L. Also, something about how "officials for years to come would be thanking them."

That was when it clicked.

When there's a disaster, people panic. They're used to having someone to look up to for answers in difficult situations. During the crisis, anyone who knows even remotely what they're doing becomes important. Global warming could eventually destroy entire civilizations, and send people around the world into mass panic. But if there were some who were already prepared, they would soon come to be relied on, and thus be able to gain power and control, fast. And what better way to prepare than to initiate the panic yourselves?

"Ahem."

I turned around to find a man in SWAT-like apparel

standing in front of the hole I had made earlier. His hand hovered threateningly over his gun holster.

It seemed as if my learning time had come to an end.

"Hands where I can see 'em," said the man. "We don't want this to get messy before the rest of the team gets here."

I didn't say anything about Global Warming being the definition of messy. Instead, I played the innocent card. "I'm so sorry for intruding!" I said. "See, I'm looking for a new home for Coding Club. I didn't realize this place was already taken."

The man narrowed his eyes. "Sure, girly. Now, I don't know what you've seen, but I'm going to need you to come with me. The boss will have some…questions."

"The boss?" I asked. I had to keep him talking until I thought of a plan. Luckily, being a logically programmed android, it didn't take me long.

"Sir, do you think that I could unplug my USB? Don't want to do anymore damage, right?" I asked.

He looked uneasy before finally nodding. "Fine. But slowly."

I reached back over my shoulder and dug my fingernail under the first solar cell I touched. It broke off with a soft click. Only twenty nine more panels to go. I continued to break off cells. I was only fourteen short of my objective when the man finally pulled his phaser on me.

"Okay, that's enough," he said.

"Just one second. I think the cord's stuck."

He strode towards me. "I said, that's enough!"

I dragged my fingernails down my arm, panels popping off. I had successfully disassembled the necessary amount of panels right before he slammed me into the wall.

Anytime now.

"You're coming with me, bot," he snarled.

SELF DESTRUCT PROTOCOL: ACTIVATED

Finally.

The man's head snapped around the room, eyes searching. "What was that?"

Even with my quickly draining energy, I managed to maneuver my lips into something that resembled a smirk. Soon, even that would be impossible. Self-destruction took a lot out of an android.

Viv had insisted on me having a self-destruct protocol. Something about it being an "android's rite of passage." I had never appreciated her insistence more.

I'm not really sure what happened to the facility after I blew up. I no longer had a body to sense with. All my files had been wirelessly transferred to the backup drive in my dorm.

Sure, I'd eventually get a new body. I hoped it would be as efficient as the last one. But hey, a body could wait. There was work to be done.

Angelique Hoffman
Thurston High School, 12th Grade

I Want

I want to draw the hearts
I want to release the
Spirit of anger
To diminish the habit of
Judgment
To draw the roses within
Oneself
That only grows in an untouched
Meadow
Overflowing of evergreen
Enjoying our roots and
Connections
Woven between us all
Loving
Without difficulty
Using our heart to
Mediate between our mind and hands

Trish Robison

Classroom Teacher
Phoenix Program at John Serbu Youth Campus

Gerald

Gerald finished the last of his spicy scorpion, slurping the tail into his mouth. He ran his hand through his short gray hair, not realizing that some of the hot sauce was still on his fingers. He walked into the cold, poorly tiled bathroom, splashed water on his face, and looked into the mirror.

"I'm tired, and look old," he thought.

For the rest of the night he sat on his couch, feet resting on a brown leather ottoman, watching Harry Potter and smelling faintly of scorpion.

Anice Teel
Thurston High School, 12th Grade

Early Morning

I believe in the sun breaking above the
horizon in the early morning. I believe
in the sound of sweet soft birds chirping and
my calm mother humming. I believe in the
smell of freshly ground and brewed dark
coffee, in the huff and rush of my sister
flying through the house in preparation for
school. I believe in the long hushed drive
to school with forlorn faces. I believe in
the dull red poles in boisterous halls
piercing voices reverberate through open breezeways.
I believe in the sick taste in my mouth
from a breakfast too early eaten.
I believe in the rustling touch of lined
paper with pencil scrawling along where
graphite becomes letters then becoming words.

Madison Smith
Thurston High School, 12th Grade

Piece Name

I want to draw a future I've never seen,
One where happiness flows like a river,
Reaching everyone around it as if
Crashing against the shore.

I'd like to draw dawn, in all its stillness,
Its forgiving gaze on the world around it.
I want the soft warmth of the morning
Sun to cast new light on all before it,
Welcoming it to be alive.

I want to draw freedom in a blaze
Of bright passion, forging a fresh,
New path on the ground below it.

Paige Davis
Thurston High School, 12th Grade

Alive

We pour our milk and honey
Beginning our morning
Our bodies become alive

Beyond the windows earth is alive
The bees work for their honey
Love birds sing good morning

Life goes; we lose that morning
That last drop of honey
So that we miss that feeling, alive

Rylan Larsen
Crow High School, 12th grade

A Dream at Death's Door: The Long Flight

Michael hopped out of his automobile into the frigid February air. He pulled his hat down over his ears to protect his shaved head from the icy stabs of the winter wind. Checking his watch, he rushed down the sidewalk and into the building. The woman at the front desk barely looked up from the bright screen in front of her as she asked him his name and date of birth. He answered, trying to hide the uneasiness in his voice.

"You're a little bit late, so just sit down and someone will be right out to take you to Dr. Bradley."

Dr. Bradley…the name sounded oddly familiar. Strange, he thought, I haven't seen this surgeon before. Maybe it's just a common name.

He thanked the woman and did as he was ordered, snatching a magazine from the waiting room coffee table on his way. He halfheartedly thumbed through the pages of a *TIME* magazine, but his focus was on other things. Surgery was the main topic eating away at him; much like the cancer in his body was causing him to waste away. The doctors told him that the treatment was not working as they had intended and the tumor was threatening to spread through his body. The three months of constant doctor visits, treatments, and shaving his head, and the countless nights when the hours of nausea and vomiting outnumbered the hours of sleep, had all been for nothing. Maybe if they just take out this tumor, he thought, the rest of the treatment will go smoother.

As he was flipping through the magazine, an advertisement caught his eye. It was a picture of a family sitting together at the dinner table. It made Michael think of his own family. He had insisted that they stay home during his surgery, telling them he would be fine and they could just come see him after he woke up. The real reason he didn't want them there was that he couldn't stand the look on their faces when they saw him in his weakened state. He couldn't bear the thought that he might not be there to protect and provide for them. He had to be strong for them. He had to fight for them.

Just then a nurse walked into the waiting room holding a metal clipboard.

"Michael?"

"Michael. Hey Mike, wake up." A man whispered sharply in his ear and shook him until he opened his eyes.

"Hey, it's your turn," whispered the owner of the dirt-covered appendage currently clamped to his shoulder. John—or "Doc" as they had nicknamed him—stared back at Mike with his bright blue eyes. These sapphire pools were a bright speck of color in an otherwise dim world. All color on this godforsaken island had been wiped out by the B-29s, tanks, and grenades. What remained after this destruction was a pitiful sight: a gray wasteland of rock and sand riddled with bomb craters and foxholes.

Mike climbed partway out of his foxhole and scanned the darkness in front of him, looking for any signs of enemy soldiers. He made sure to keep low, in case the Japanese were doing the same from the protection of their complex system of tunnels. Just three days on the island had made him alert, paranoid almost. He would jump at every nighttime noise, half-expecting the enemy to pop out one of these tunnels in front of him. Any changes in the smell of the salty, smoky air would make his heart skip. And when he saw—there! His entire body grew tense and he slid his calloused finger into the trigger guard. About 60 yards up the face of the mountain, there was movement. It was slow and methodical, creeping along ever so gently. Mike raised his rifle to locate the entity with his scope, and when he did, he identified the object as…a cloud of mist. He let out a quiet sigh of relief and lowered his rifle. This was not the first time he had mistaken nightly vapors for an enemy assassin, and it certainly wouldn't be the last.

    He absentmindedly rubbed his prickly scalp, and in doing so, realized that he had forgotten his helmet in the foxhole. It was a stupid mistake, but luckily it was not a costly one… this time. He groped around in the dark pit until his hand hit the cloth-covered steel bowl, which he then snatched up and slid over his skull. The protection provided by the metal hat gave him a sense of safety that lasted for the remainder of his watch. He woke Doc and settled back into his sand-covered sleeping mat. For five minutes he laid there, thinking about the challenges of the day ahead. There would be shooting, blood, and death, but he had to be resilient to lead his men to victory.

    The nurse led him down the long trench of curtained rooms until eventually showing him to his own. The pre-op room was cold and sterile, with gray stone tile and a white bed—not the stress-relieving atmosphere Michael had hoped for. Once he had changed into the hospital gown, the nurse returned and settled him into the padded, metal-railed cot she called a bed. After that, she poked him with needles and hooked him up to a screen that hummed and showed several sets of numbers. Not too long after, a man in a white coat slid the curtain open and walked in. The bright blue tie around his neck stood out against the blank background that was his shirt.

The man—Dr. Bradley—asked Michael some questions, listened to his heart, and then gave him a pill to help him relax. This relaxation was short-lived because moments later, Dr. Bradley was holding Michael's X-rays up to the pale light with a perplexed look on his face. The doctor whispered something to the nurse and she scurried out of the room. He then turned to Michael and informed him that they weren't certain, but it was possible the cancer had already spread.

Michael's heart pounded as the questions poured out. Where had the cancer spread? Why hadn't they caught this sooner? What would happen now? He was panicking, and he needed answers, but Dr. Bradley didn't seem to have any. A while later, Michael calmed himself down—as much as he could, anyway—and he prepared himself for whatever would happen next. The Doc handed him a clipboard with some papers to sign, and Mike trembled anxiously as he signed and initialed the empty spaces. When the nurse returned, her eyes were down and her shoulders were rigid. She whispered to the doctor yet again, and the doctor relayed the information to Mike. His arms went limp and his fists unclenched, sending the clipboard clattering to the floor.

Ra-ta-ta-ta-tat!
In one swift motion, Mike snatched up his helmet and

rifle, and leapt to his feet in the shallow sand hole. Bullets cut through the sky above, and the shouts of men—both American and Japanese—were beginning to fill the air. The wounded were crying out for the doctor while the leaders called out orders. Mike scanned the mountainside, keeping a wary eye out for the enemy while searching for his men. Finding John, he barked out his own orders to move up and keep firing. The look in John's perceptive blue eyes told Mike he understood. John then turned and hollered to some men below him who were concealed from their sergeant's sight.

Mike returned his attention to the looming mountain in front of him. He needed to advance, and he needed to advance now. Movement in the bunker just ahead of him drew his attention. It was only a split second, but that was all it took. The brief glimpse of the star soldered onto the front of the steel helmet told Mike that it was an enemy soldier. He reached down to his waist and pulled a grenade from his belt. Pulling the pin, he waited—one thousand…two thousand…three thousand. Then in the nick of time, he tossed the grenade into the bunker twenty yards up the hill. The explosion rumbled beneath his feet, and a plume of dusty smoke shot into the air.

He moved quickly, laying down cover fire as he went. He reached the bunker in less than eight seconds, and, inspecting the crater, concluded that no life remained. The bunker was positioned about halfway up the mountain, so it would give Mike a great place to shout orders to his men and…

"帝国のために！"

He turned in time to see an enemy soldier pop out of one of the many secret tunnels embedded in the mountain. To Mike's dismay, this particular tunnel opened right into the bunker he currently occupied. Both soldiers instinctively whipped their guns to their shoulder and fired. One shot was all it took, and the man crumpled before him. The life drained out of him quickly, soaking into the sand beneath him. Mike's stomach turned, as it always did, watching the consequence of his necessary action take place before him. He placed his hand over his abdomen—trying to stay the queasiness—and found that it was moist. Mike's eyes followed the trail of buttons down his torso and came to rest on the ever widening scarlet patch just to the right of his navel. His knees suddenly became weak, and he fell to the ground. A ringing began in his right ear, and dark rings enclosed his vision. The darkness was closing in around him, and he managed one last cry:

"Doc!!"

"Doctor Bradley?!" A woman's voice fretfully rang out. Michael opened his eyes and looked around at the sterile operating room. Everything was so strange, so surreal and hazy. Tubes and strange-looking instruments protruded from his stomach, and a machine was beeping frantically to his right.

"Doctor Bradley. Blood pressure's dropping." The anxiety was building in her voice. Should he be anxious? Was something wrong?

"Heart rate is increasing." Michael locked eyes with the nurse, who then quickly reported his state of consciousness to the doctor.

"Get a clamp on that artery, get him some more fluids, and someone get him under for Pete's sake!"

Everything felt as though he was in a dream. Of course, that could have been caused by the anesthetic. But what if he was dreaming? Or what if he just woke from the dream? The awful shooting and bleeding and dying could also be a figment of his imagination. Mike continued contemplating this as the nurse injected something into the IV. As everything around him began to grow dim, he could feel himself being lifted up. The shadows of five figures surrounded him, lifting the makeshift stretcher out of bunker. It seemed quiet, and as Mike looked around, he understood why—most of the shooting had stopped. Hundreds of soldiers, both Japanese and American, had given their lives for their countries, and their sacrifice covered the battlefield. He took a moment to remember the men whose bodies lay still on the field below him.

"Hey Sarge." Mike turned his eyes away from the depressing sight and saw Doc looking back at him.

"We found a way to the top. This is our chance to take the high ground, but we gotta leave now." His company turned to him, searching for his go-ahead. He saw hope in their eyes—a rare sight on the death-abundant island. He nodded, and they continued up the mountain, keeping a sharp eye out for the Japanese tunnels. With them they carried the flag, the symbol of bravery, freedom, and hope. He could almost feel the pride radiating from his men with each step they took. It was at that moment Mike realized he needed to stand with his men. He had to be strong and lead them to victory, for they had seen enough death and despair that day.

Mike commanded his men to stop, and he carefully swung his legs over the side of the flimsy stretcher. His feet crunched into the rocky soil as he tried to stand, and the dark rings around his vision returned, threatening to cover him in darkness.

As he collapsed to his knees, he found himself in the hospital yet again. This time, though, he saw himself from above, sitting in his hospital bed surrounded by his family. There was a smile on his face, for the doctor had given them good news:

the surgery had worked. The fight was far from over, yet as the Doc informed them of Mike's treatment options, the look on his family members' faces told him he would get through it.

The vision faded and he looked up to see his men, Harlon, Ira, Frank, Rene, and the medic—his savior—John H. Bradley. They were looking at him, willing him to stand, to stand with them and take the mountain. He realized now that this was real, more real than anything ever was or will be. The fight was not over yet, but as long as his brothers were there to stand with him, they could push through whatever obstacles got in their way.

Mustering his strength, Mike pushed himself off the ground and stood.

"Whatcha waitin' for, we got a flag to raise."

Melissa Rendsland
Thurston High School, 12th Grade

I Believe

I believe in small drops of rain plinking
melodically from roof to ground in the dark evening.
I believe in sipping coffee with its bold,
bitter taste after the sweet richness of a donut.
I believe in the sweet gush of minty insides,
wrapped in smooth chocolate.
I believe in cool, cloudy breezes hitting your face
through the window of a warm house.
I believe in clinking metallic sounds,
the exertion of muscles as pain rips through.
I believe in the crisp click, pop, fizz of smooth,
bubbly liquid caffeine running across your tongue.
I believe in the tinkling of freedom hanging
from a woven lanyard around your neck.
I believe in the buzzing of the thick,
hot air as small drops cut through cooling your skin.

Dan Renteria
Thurston High School, 12th Grade

Boring

It's like a nail hitting the floor.
The floor is wet because
The mop went over it.
The mop went back into the closet,
The janitor went home to sleep.
He's dreaming of not mopping.
Does the floor want to be mopped?
Maybe the mop is tired of mopping
And doesn't want to mop anymore.
Maybe it wants a haircut,
Maybe it wants its own bedroom,
Maybe the mop doesn't want to be a mop.
Who knows?
Mops don't talk…
At least to us.

Matthew Johnson
Thurston High School, 12th Grade

Concentration

Yes, I am small, unimportant and insignificant, people often overlook me along with everything else, and fail to realize I am here, at least when I am alone. But when I'm a part of you, *I* becomes *we*, and we bloom a path of new lessons, and write new records of "the best."

But you never know I, alone, am there, only that we are here.

Blake McKay
Thurston High School, 12th Grade

Be

Breathe
The world is alive
No hands on the wheel, eyes closed for the future
Only the touch of the present dictates
The taste of the now
The taste might be nourishing
It might be stingy
You can dream of the future
But it's what you do now
You will fall
You will hurt
That's living in the world
It's life, it's real
The world is wide
But you are at advantage
It can drag it
It's the light that comes out of soul
You can be loved, you can differentiate
You can be anything you want in the now
You are the now

Angelique Hoffman
Thurston High School, 12th Grade

Blind Directions

1. Follow the windy cracked roads you used to hate
2. Listen for the soothing stream of the river where your favorite book was read
3. Make sure to pass the big green fields and the local market that stinks of grease
4. Feel the suffocating energy, something so familiar
5. You are almost there, the tiny gray town
6. I said I would never come back, but I found my mind wandering here

Alex Johnson
Thurston High School, 12th Grade

Restlessness

I lie there awake, with
my mind racing as fast as electricity.
I close my eyes and listen
to the rain hitting the roof,
the thunder roaring in the wind,
the lightning cracking
in the distance.
It's like God doesn't want me
to sleep tonight. Tossing
and turning, never seeming
to get comfortable. Burning
hot like the midday
sun.

Charlie Schneider

Writer in Residence
Phoenix Program at John Serbu Youth Campus

Excerpt from "Heyday"

When she's not humming over the news or rocking in a church pew, Mom is sitting there in the living room looking out the window at our corner all day like it's going to look different than it did the day before, the decade before. She sits there with her pumice stone grinding her feet away and waits for a disaster to visit the neighborhood all at once. She thinks it's going to be big, like a meteor shower, or a bulldozer at least, but she's deluded. Death here is slow as a broken gutter puddling up the sidewalk, drip by drip. You barely see it, and then in six months there's no sidewalk.

But then, she's tending more toward fantasy lately. When I'm in the kitchen fixing her a couple slices of tomato with salt and pepper, which is all she eats now, I hear her muttering. I know what's coming. She likes to think she does, too.

"Dead heat simmering," she says. "Drought. A famine out in the hinterlands. Then a blizzard. Then a flood. A tornado, picking up Grand River Avenue and slamming it down like a little runt's fist when he wants lunch. Then a volcano downtown, and a giant sinkhole gapes open in Dearborn. Cars, schools, highways, and neighborhoods, and the Ford HQ, down they go, pills down a throat. Disease rolls into town in an old Cadillac Calais and starves us, wanders us from store to store, our eyes cross each other, nothing fills us even halfway, and then an earthquake stops in. Churns us. Shuffles us all up, makes the city a milkshake in a blender for three minutes and we're all screaming, and our bellies are rumbling the whole time, but you can't hear them because the empty shelves are rattling, and plus then the fires start. They come in from nowhere and sweep into our vacants, and the smoke and the fire from the all our vacants gets swept into downtown, and the smoke and the heat from downtown pours down into the river, which boils the boats, the swimmers, and the fishes, and then a tidal wave comes in, mad and uninvited. It's coming toward you so fast you can't even shit. And you want to, because there's never been a tidal wave on the Detroit River in all recorded history, but there it is getting bigger in your own God-given eyes until your whole vision turns gray-black and then black-black, blacker than your deepest secret, which is pretty damn black, I know, because you grew up stealing my quarters and probably only got worse from there. But then an asteroid shows up. It's racing down, and there's a solar flare rising—"

"Jesus A. Christ, Mom," I say, "shut up already, for love, money, or—"

"Or for some *g-d quiet*, I know, sweetheart, I know. You'll get your quiet."

I try to remind myself she's got business sense and a killer instinct. I know she's poking me. I know she's poking me to get at me and yet still I rise to it and tell her to shut up, which some might suggest I shouldn't do. But they haven't lived with Mom for 45 years. She's been on about disasters since Pops bit it, and remarkably, the list isn't quite the same every time. You wouldn't know how many kinds of natural disasters there are unless you've got a deeply morbid mind, and my mother's mind is bent like Tammy Geraldson's back is bent.

But we have to have compassion for Tammy, who we see hunched under vent shafts all over town. Tammy got a place on some gymnast team back in the day, but she failed her first of what became quite a few drug tests. Now she has a cardboard medal hanging down under her buzzard neck. "Distinguished Service," it says, but I don't know what service she ever did. And then it says "Spare change for words" just below that. You give her change out of curiosity, and she tells you something like you're right and honorable and that we should all be so lucky to exhibit such charity by the sunset of our days.

Mom rolls Tammy out to me all the time, and to Mom I say Grant Cochrane. He's the janitor at her church who said someone slammed a door on his pinkie and severed it. Really, he cut it off for the disability insurance money. He claimed that as a janitor, the injury "significantly impaired his ability to do the manual labor involved in pastoral upkeep," and I don't know which two-dime lawyer fed him that line, but it worked. The insurance people believed him. So I ask Mom: should we have compassion for him? He's not suffering. He's fine. He's got income.

Mom says he is a man, and every man has his own pain, and that leads him to sin. Six months ago, he got a loan from us to buy his wife a necklace after she found out he cheated on her with her sister. His wife accepted the necklace and wore it all the way up to the front desk of Jimmy's Discount Jackpot, where she pawned it for an undisclosed sum. Then she got some divorce papers drawn up for cheap, and Cochrane hasn't moved from his barstool since. But Pastor Richie continues to pay Sinner Man Cochrane to dust and mop and clean toilets and organize hymnals just like he did before. Grant Cochrane is pinkie-less, and he's perfectly competent. He's swindling the insurance people and the church. Yes, Mom says, and I don't know what she means by that.

Right before he tapped out, Pops did say something sensible. He told Mom that churchgoing was about as useful as knocking on the front door of one of our Hyacinth Avenue vacants.

"Rhoda, you can knock and knock," he said, "but all you'll hear is knocking."

Then he died, and Mom added her Tuesday mornings. She's thinking of adding Thursdays now, too. When I asked her why she had to go to church so much, she said there was no greater privilege on Earth. She's really lost it for God, like the Man's going to knock back. She's the happiest person I know.

Matthew Johnson
Thurston High School, 12th Grade

Deer of Stone

A dotted body and head, without eyes—blind,
but still has not lost vision of what we can see
through our ancestor's minds.

As time brushes forward for us,
what we choose to leave behind
is a picture of our eyes from the hand
of creativity.

Parker B. Rook
Thurston High School, 12th Grade

Dread

That's it, stuck in a seven foot hole in the ground.
Brothers on both sides not bound by blood.
Everything is loud, from the rats to no man's land.
The coarse grinding of gears and treads.
An ironclad tank trudges overhead.
It won't survive long.
Gas masks don't stop the smell.
Even without expression we look scared.
Boys fight for men.
Nothing great about it.

Paige Davis
Thurston High School, 12th Grade

My Life to Be

I want to draw a future I've never seen
Where small extensions of me giggle
And play with sunburnt faces
And purpled knees
I'll draw bright blues and greens
And yellows in their eyes and
Little sun kisses across their
Cheeks and shoulders
I'll draw puppies and ponies
A dozen for each
And friends who explore all day
Looking for fun and
Finding adventure

Doran Simpson
Thurston High School, 12th Grade

Confusion

A resident of your own personal dream world
You return to reality too late
Your instructions have already been given
Your task is at hand in front of you
But you do not see it, for you don't
Know what it is you're looking for
Your time is all used up now
And you still haven't even begun

Abrial Vinson
Thurston High School, 12th Grade

Five Directions to My House

Go through the roundabout and turn on Daisy Street
Drive until you see the Pink House
The dead rose bush and yellow grass will lead you
The broken pavement will guide you
The dull brass door knob will let you in

Sander Moffitt
Roosevelt Middle School, 8th grade

Seeking the Hidden

On the 25th of July, the day before my seventh birthday, Mickie's Pet Mart burned down. Not that it was ever a high-quality establishment, with walls of eroded concrete just barely containing its limited collection of leopard geckos and boxes upon boxes of crickets awaiting their inevitable deaths. A lone fan pushed perpetually on, suspended from the ceiling by an unstable chain. The small establishment rarely had visitors, much less regulars. Almost nobody noticed its disappearance. But I did, because to a six-year-old, such an event is a big deal. I didn't spend any time wondering what would happen to Mickie, nor why exactly the store had burned, but about a specific animal that called the mini-mart its home. An old, sickly green macaw.

The avian, which responded only to the name Frank, wasn't in what my father would call "Vending Condition." A long scar marred his lower beak, carving deep into the keratin in a suspiciously knife-like stroke. He had constant tics, from a twitching of his head to a crook in his wing that would repeat until it stuck. Whoever was assigned to the unfortunate task of assisting Mickie that day would get the trusty ladder from its usual place behind the register—where it was kept for such occasions, as Frank rarely went a day without needing it—and ascend to the macaw's roost.

Frank kept his nest on a small ledge just inside the store,

high to the left of the door. His abode was crafted from old newspaper clippings of the funnies. One of the old assistants, a quiet man who went only by the name of Williams, used to trim them from *The Rising Star*, our local paper, and pin them to the corkboard that hung behind the gecko cages. Every Sunday, just like clockwork, he'd bring the paper in and remove a special pair of sewing scissors from the register's $5 bill slot. The intricately carved golden tool would slide along the edges of the comics and they'd fall to the ground in a slow, sloping drift. Every Sunday, he'd pin them up, and by each Monday they'd be gone and Frank's crib would be decked out in the current newspaper-dull colors.

For some reason, Mickie found this to be the funniest thing in the universe. A deep laugh would rumble from a place lower than her stomach, and would persist long into the night, as the mini-mart didn't close until three. "Ain't that the darndest thing," she'd laugh. "Ain't it?" Williams never commented. But he kept on with the funnies, with their dully colored comics and overused catchlines.

When I was tracking down Mickie's old employees to write this article, I found quite the variety in life. A Hispanic woman by the name of Dorothy went on to become a dental nurse. The man I remember always smoked cigarettes behind the counter married a business shark and they adopted triplet girls. Lori Kenneth, just seven years older than I am, is now working at a McDonalds. They all refused to speak with me. But Williams? His body was found in a black Nissan Altima fifty miles south of our town border three years ago. Nobody even noticed he was gone.

My six-year-old self didn't notice any of this. The only thing I wondered was where Frank would go. As it turned out, that didn't seem to be much of a problem. The macaw, along with the rest of the animals, died in the fire.

For a few glorious minutes after smoke ceased to billow violently from the small building, all I could picture was Frank winning. At that point I didn't understand exactly how flames ravage a body. I imagined him rising through the fire like a phoenix, flames engulfing him as his majestic wings spread to accept and invite the blaze. As if he was saying, *Burn me. Do it. Just you try.* For a few glorious minutes, this was what I pictured. Then the firemen left the building a smoky husk of its previous self, and as my dad went to talk to them, I snuck in.

Nothing was the same. The geckos were gone, with only crisped ashes in the ruins of their cages remaining. I should've known then. The geckos were placed right next to the heating vents.

I almost threw up at the crickets. They were kept in small boxes with mesh lids. Something dark protruded from each and every gap, blocking the airways. At first, I thought it was ash or cinders or some form of smoke, maybe melted plastic. As I approached, though, my stomach turned over and my heart stopped.

Crickets' heads. They were crickets' heads, stuck desperately through the holes in their cage as they tried to escape, tried to leap from their dying home.

I stumbled back and sat down hard, hands clasped over my legs, trying anything to keep from losing it. An unsettled air had spread the instant I entered, but I think it was in this exact moment that it evolved from unsettled to mania.

My dad ran in at that point, and his arms latched under mine as he dragged me from the mini pet mart, frantically trying to maintain my innocence. But that didn't stop me from seeing Frank's burned body, angry red patches ripping where green belly feathers should have lain. His beak, completely broken off at the scar. His wings were the worst, though. Bent at all the wrong angles, white bone peeking out from under burned, bloodied flesh.

Not a phoenix at all.

It wasn't until eight years later I started to wonder about why the mart burned down.

At that point, I was just entering ninth grade in a new town. We'd moved a few months after the fire, two towns over, to give me a fresh start. A fact strewn into the room by a trivia-crazy math teacher would be the start of my investigation. One in twelve people have been convicted of a felony.

A seemingly innocent piece of information, one mixed among such randomly tossed comments as Captain Crunch's full name is Horatio Magellan Crunch and -40° Fahrenheit is the same temperature as -40° Celsius. But it stuck with me. I began to look at people differently, examining each face I passed. Did a bigger nose signify a felony? Blue eyes? Dyed hair? Knuckles shrouded in rings? I thought back to each town I'd lived in, a whopping total of six by the age of fourteen. In each town, I knew at least twelve people.

I thought past Wiscon, where I currently live, to towns I'd mostly forgotten. Altha, where I'd lived briefly at the age of twelve. Garcon Point when I was ten. Hosford at nine. Lloyd at seven. For the first time in years, I thought back to my town of birth, Chumuckla, and the pet store where I'd seen too much.

As a little kid, I'd never been able to properly pronounce Chumuckla. Chooom-klu, I'd run around the house screeching joyfully. Chooooooooomklu! My kindergarten teachers loved it. Any of them could have been convicted of a felony.

From there, my mind hopped immediately to the mini-mart, where I'd spend my after-school hours. Even as a little kid, I remembered every single detail about those people that worked there. Dorothy was an incredibly delicate woman with a long, pinched face and thin, plain brown hair. She always had lollipops in her back pockets and would never neglect to give me one, even when I'd already obviously had sugar that day. Lori Kenneth was a naïve girl with beach-blonde hair and a chest too large for her own good. Lack in judgement is what eventually drove her from the pet haven. Miguel, who would run through a pack of smokes a day, sported ripped black muscle shirts and a pencil mustache but melted at the geckos. For some reason, Miguel had an emotional affair with the animals. His favorite, his *bella*, he would call her, was a soft, intricate leopard gecko with a thick tail and eyes that wondered. I played with that leopard gecko on the floor of the pet mart every Tuesday and Thursday after three forty-five. One day, I sat by the heater as the gecko climbed her rocky course up my arm, and a series of sharp clicks rang through the panels. Her claws dug into my leg and drew blood, but I didn't move. Miguel was over in seconds, lifting the animal to safety and bandaging my calf, offering me candy. I never told anyone how I got the perfectly oval scars just in the shape of gecko talons.

 Any of them could have been convicted, but if my money had to go on someone, it would've been Mickie herself. Monster of a woman, maybe in her early sixties, massive, with a variety of ratty paisley headscarves wrapped around her head. Undereye bags bluer than her hair. Loud, bright fabrics always almost wriggled with life against her body. A motherly figure, with soft fat instead of smooth curve, but she would never dress in fewer than ten individual colors. Bright red pencil heels and massive patterned skirts burst from underneath her working apron. I'd only heard her full name once, given by a new employee on the first day. Michelle Martinez. It just didn't fit the way Mickie did.

No matter how crazed she was on any particular day, Mickie always found time for me, to play with me. She boasted a very clean apron every time, despite the consistent mess of the pet shop. She maintained a whack sense of humor, and a scratchy, cracking voice, and always had a certain flashing in her eyes that made people respect her. As she stepped outside to grab something from her car, not a minute before the fire began, I noticed a huge gray stain on her smock. I've never seen her since.

When I went to look for her, to write this article, it was as if she'd never existed. There were no records of a Michelle Martinez living anywhere in Florida, much less owning a pet store. The mini-mart had no webpage, no advertising, no means of recognition. It sat nestled between a dying laundromat and a decaying casino on the East Side. So when digital records didn't turn anything up, I persuaded my dad to take a day trip down to Chumuckla.

The excuse I gave was nostalgia, something to which the parents of kids who move a lot are sympathetic. I claimed a want to visit the old preschool playground, knowing full well how boring he found the place. He arranged to have lunch at a friend's house while I reminisced, then I would come over when I was ready to leave.

There are three fundamental steps to solving a mystery, according to WikiHow. Collecting data, forming a hypothesis, and proving a conclusion. The only data I had were the memories of a six-year-old, which were about as reliable as public transport. I figured I merited a trip to the place where it all began.

My dad was extremely cautious the day of. He checked and triple-checked that I had all I would need, from my phone to snacks, though I assured him I'd only be gone a few hours. He made me swear to stay near the school, and under no circumstances wander anywhere near the mini-mart. Crossed fingers still work for ninth graders.

From the outside, the squat building still appeared the same. Same whitewashed exterior, more patched cracks than concrete. Fire only ravaged the gut of the store. A huge crack webbed across the glass window in the door, which hung slightly at an angle. As I pushed it open, a grinding, screeching creak drilled from the imbalanced hinges and I winced as I stepped inside.

The memories all came rushing back in a blur. All the times spent with Miguel and his geckos, Dorothy and her lollipops. How Lori would strut in to work with her arm slung around a new guy each week, and the progressing air of exhaustion that floated in with her. Mostly of Mickie, though. All of the details I'd forgotten. How she smelled of minty pine, the gum she chewed ceaselessly. Her barrettes that held the bandanna in place shaped like a small silver bird. The yellow pouch of mixed nuts that hung at her waist. When I was hungry we'd spread the types on the counter and she'd show me which were safe to eat and which weren't. In hindsight, it was probably a safety hazard to have a little kid discerning between poisonous nuts and edible ones. If I correctly remembered the good ones, she'd let me have a few.

My fingers drifted along the melted counter, which hadn't been replaced since the fire. Almost nothing had. I was looking for some record of people that had worked there. Nothing. Two hours spent going through the metal drawers under the desk that had survived the fire, and I couldn't even come up with a nametag. The closest thing I found to Mickie was a small strip of the ugly yellow leather that made up the nut bag. I clenched it tightly in my palm until my nails dug below my skin.

Charred husks of crates and old treats sat strewn everywhere with no rhyme or reason. I didn't even try to find signs of anyone in the mess that was the gecko cages. I didn't dare near the crickets. Frank's ledge was long gone, stripped away, probably, in the aftermath of the fire.

As I was leaving, though, something caught my eye. A flash of white just above where his nest used to be. Better judgement warned me that it was a bad idea, that I'd injure myself, but I hauled the rickety old ladder out from where it sat behind the desk and dragged it over.

Every ascending step was a challenge. The entire thing nearly gave out at rung six, when my foot slipped to the edge and crashed straight through the rotten wood. A small shriek escaped my lips as I scurried up. It turned out to be worth it ten times over, though.

The smallest sliver of a Brazil nut hung stabbed into the wall by a bright red tack. I was going to dismiss it, just leave it, but as I was climbing down something swung out from behind.

I pulled the tack from the wall and dropped it carefully to the ground, the shaving of Brazil nut still pressed between my fingers. The tiny piece of folded paper fluttered into my outstretched palm.

Upon reaching the ground again, I exited the small shop and sat down on the curb like I used to in kindergarten. My fingers shook as I struggled to uncrease the tiny folds in the slip of paper until it finally yielded. Inside was a comic strip.

The comic, which I immediately recognized from the old

Sunday funnies in *The Rising Star*, portrayed a woman who looked eerily like Mickie. Miguel and I used to joke about it all the time. Her speech bubble rose just above her towering pile of hair—which we used to joke Mickie would kill for—was scratched out with a black pen, and chicken scratch lettering floated above.

She's a monster

Signed in tiny print in the bottom right corner, just under the woman's shoe, was a small letter: *W*.

Three horizontal lines sat scratched into the paper's background, and suddenly it was all too clear. I dashed into the blackened mini-mart, sprinted over to the back wall, and ripped the heating grate from the wall. There was no vent, but a passage large enough for a person. I crawled along desperately, praying, hoping it wasn't true. Step Two: Form a hypothesis. I had hoped mine would be proven false.

Soon enough, the remainder of the ugly yellow pouch came into view, nuts still spilling from its brim. Three had bite-sized chunks missing. Three of the nuts I was told were poisonous for me to eat.

I crawled as quickly as I could along the building's artery, my heart hammering against my ribs, praying that I was wrong.

A single green feather rested strewn in the middle of the path. I closed my eyes and kept going. The passage opened up into a room that wouldn't be there were this a normal vent. My heart dropped.

Dead birds. The room was filled with cages upon cages of dead birds. Locks hung messily from each cage, as if arranged by a crazy person, a frenetic person. A gray paste clung to the wings of some, pressing them to their bodies, and when I leaned in to take a whiff the scent of pine flooded through me. Step Three: Proving a conclusion. Shit.

And now, as I'm sitting here writing this, I think back to everything I missed. Frank's flightlessness. Williams's constant fear. The pine "gum," The inedible nuts. I was spending my time with a smuggler.

I think wikiHow was wrong. There aren't three steps to solving a mystery, but four. Step Four: Dealing with what you've learned.

This article is one of many in my diary. Who knows who'll end up reading it eventually, or if anyone will ever find Mickie, or what exactly happened to Williams, but whatever happens, I know the truth. And this just confirms what I already knew: Ignorance can truly be bliss.

Carter McKenzie

Writer in Residence
Thurston High School, 12th Grade

What Must Be True

keep the strange book you have chosen
open

your willingness
toward its emptiness

not yours
and yours

the table before you
nothing

suspended
over the distances

your desire of signals
your willingness toward

what may live
in darkness

fragment after
fragment nothing

you can keep

what may become
hidden tracks

unbound

    the running deer
    beyond the window   her dark

    what can never
      be found

      the green world
          of that window

    signaling

the bright road
of rain

leading to the house
not here but made

of that rain
the door left open

at the bottom of the childhood stairs

so you might see her

the sharpness
of light

what might stay with you

light deepening

the shadows of branches
you cannot see

shaping the field of the page
the imprint

the calling

what must be true

    given

you keep following

www.ingramcontent.com/pod-product-compliance
Lightning Source LLC
LaVergne TN
LVHW040158080526
838202LV00042B/3212